D0513473

Talking
With
God

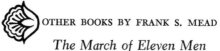 OTHER BOOKS BY FRANK S. MEAD

The March of Eleven Men
Who's Who in the Bible
Ten Decisive Battles of Christianity
See These Banners Go
Rebels with a Cause
On Our Own Doorstep
Right Here at Home
The Encyclopedia of Religious Quotations
Let Freedom Ring! (with Dale Evans Rogers)
Handbook of Denominations in the United States
Tarbell's Teacher's Guide (editor)

Talking With God

Prayers for Today

Edited by
FRANK S. MEAD

A. J. HOLMAN COMPANY
Division of J. B. Lippincott Company
Philadelphia and New York

U.S. Library of Congress Cataloging in Publication Data

Mead, Frank Spencer, birth date
Talking with God.
1. Prayers. I. Title.
BV245.M485   242'.8   75–37620
ISBN–0–87981–052–1

Special acknowledgment is made to the following people and publishers who have granted permission for the use of selections in this book:

Association Press for prayers from *Treat Me Cool, Lord*, by Carl F. Burke and from *Daily Life Prayers for Youth* by Walter L. Cook. / *Christian Herald* magazine for prayers by Norman Gale and Arminal Elizabeth Hay. / Collins Publishers for prayer by William Barclay in *Prayers for Young People*. / Concordia Publishing House for Paraphrase of Psalm 92 from *God Is Here, Let's Celebrate*, by Leslie F. Brandt, copyright 1969 by Concordia Publishing House. Used by permission. / Dodd, Mead & Company for prayer from *A Book of Prayer* by the Rev. Samuel McComb. / Hawthorn Books, Inc., for Charles Hanson Towne's "Easter Canticle" from *Selected Poems of Charles Hanson Towne*. / Herald Press for prayer for wayward children from *Breaking Bread Together*, edited by Elaine Sommers Rich, copyright 1958 by Herald Press, Scottdale, Pa. 15683. / Mrs. Gerald Jahoda for prayer by Adelaide Love. / Catherine Marshall LeSourd for prayers by Peter Marshall. / J. B. Lippincott Company for prayer by Jeanette Struchen, from *Prayers to Pray Wherever You Are*, by Jeanette Struchen, copyright © 1969 by Jeanette Struchen. Reprinted by permission of J. B. Lippincott Company. / Macmillan Publishing Company for prayer by Rabindranath Tagore from *Gitanjali*, published in the United States by Macmillan Company, Inc., 1913, and prayer from *Collective Brooding* by Robert Raines, copyright by Robert Raines, 1966, reprinted with the permission of Macmillan Publishing Company. / Methodist Publishing House, London, for two prayers from *Daily Readings*. From W. E. Sangster. / *The New Pulpit Digest* for prayer by Rita F. Snowden. / Mrs. Theo Oxenham for prayer by John Oxenham from *Bees in Amber*, published by Fleming H. Revell Company. / Fleming H. Revell Company for prayers from *Prayers for Young People* by Herman N. Beimfohr; prayer from *Mr. Jones, Meet the Master* by Peter Marshall; prayer from *If I Could Pray Again* by David A. Redding; prayer from *Prayerfully* by Helen Steiner Rice; prayer from *My Spiritual Diary* by Dale Evans Rogers; two prayers from *Prayers for Parents Who Care* and *A Book of Prayers for Youth* by John Lewis Sandlin. / Charles Scribner's Sons for prayer from *A Diary of Private Prayer* by John Baillie. / Lisa Sergio for the teenager's prayer by Wilma Curtis. / TIME Inc. for prayer by General MacArthur from *MacArthur's Rendezvous with History* by Courtney Whitney, published by Alfred A. Knopf. Copyright 1955 by TIME Inc. Reprinted with permission. / United Church Press for prayer from *Prayers of the Social Awakening* by Walter Rauschenbusch, published by Pilgrim Press, 1925. / Charles L. Wallis for prayer by J. S. Hoyland from *Masterpieces of Religious Verse*, page 349, published by Harper and Row, reprinted by permission.

 *Contents*

Lord, Teach Us to Pray

The best and the worst of us feel the urge to pray; it is a universal instinct of the soul. But too few of us know how to pray, or for what. From the prayers gathered in this book and from the pray-ers, we find at least four suggestions as to the how and what. To wit:

Pray *humbly*, never proudly. The prayer of the haughty Pharisee never got beyond the roof, but the prayer of the humble publican reached and touched the heart of God the instant it was uttered. We must pray not in pride of what we are, but in hope of what we may be, with the help of His Spirit.

Pray in *confession*; tell God all of it. Let it be even painfully honest. The least little cover-up will smother all the rest of it. Since Eden, God has never once been deceived by any of His human creatures, nor by the insincerity of any prayer.

Pray in complete *unselfishness*, for others as

well as for ourselves, asking not what we can get but what we can give. Prayer is no "gimme game" to be played with God; He gives what we need, not what we may selfishly want. It might be good to thank Him occasionally for not answering some of of our prayers with a "Yes."

Pray in *expectancy*. Why pray at all, if we doubt that He is listening? Prayer in vague hope is nothing better than vague wishing; pray in faith, and He will hear.

Such prayer changes things. Or, better, as Francis Quarles has said, "Prayer changes people, and people change things."

Prayer is both talking with God and listening for His answers, and it may just be that the listening is more important than the talking—and it also may just be that the people in this book understood that the most important moments in prayer are the first five minutes after we say "Amen."

FRANK S. MEAD

 *The Two Best-Known Prayers*

It may be that the best prayers are the shortest prayers—those that say it quickly and to the point. Two of the best-known Christian prayers are beautifully brief. One, immortal because of its source, begins,

> "Our Father, which art in heaven,
> Hallowed be Thy name. . . ."

And the other, which some call childish but which none of us seem able to forget or put out of our hearts or minds, begins,

> "Now I lay me down to sleep;
> I pray the Lord my soul to keep. . . ."

 *For the Morning*

You are ushering in another day
Untouched and freshly new,
So here I come to ask You, God,
If You'll renew me, too.
Forgive the many errors
That I made yesterday
And let me try again, dear God,
To walk closer in Thy way. . . .
But, Father, I am well aware
I can't make it on my own.
So take my hand and hold it tight
For I can't walk alone.

Helen Steiner Rice

Almighty God, who alone gavest us the breath of life, and alone canst keep alive in us the holy desires thou dost impart; We beseech thee, for thy compassion's sake, to sanctify all our thoughts and endeavours; that we may neither begin an action without a pure intention nor continue it without thy blessing. And grant that, having the eyes of the mind opened to behold things invisible and unseen, we may in heart be inspired by thy wisdom, and in work be upheld by thy strength, and in the end be accepted of thee as thy faithful servants; through Jesus Christ our Saviour. Amen.

The Book of Common Prayer

Help me, God, to make a more determined effort to at least start each day by talking intimately with You, before I wade into the rushing stream of daily chores.

Dale Evans Rogers

Let this day, O Lord, add some knowledge or good deed to yesterday.

Lancelot Andrews

Once more a new day lies before us, our Father. As we go out among men to do our work, touching the hands and lives of our fellows, make us, we pray Thee, friends of all the world. Save us from blighting the fresh flower of any heart by the flare of sudden anger or secret hate. May we not bruise the rightful self-respect of any by contempt or malice. Help us to cheer the suffering by our sympathy, to freshen the drooping of our hopefulness, and to strengthen in all the wholesome sense of worth and the joy of life. Save us from the deadly poison of class pride. Grant that we may look all men in the face with the eyes of a brother. If any needs us, make us ready to yield our help, ungrudgingly unless higher duties claim us, and may we rejoice that we have it in us to be helpful to our fellowmen.

Walter Rauschenbusch

Father, I thank Thee for Thy mercies, which are new every morning. For the gift of sleep; for health and strength; for the vision of another day with its fresh opportunities of work and service; for all these and more than these, I thank Thee. Before looking on the face of men I would look upon Thee, Who art the health of my countenance and my God. Not without Thy guidance would I go

forth to meet the duties and the tasks of the day.
Strengthen me so that in all my work I may be
faithful; amid trials, courageous; in suffering,
patient; under disappointment, full of hope in
Thee. Grant this for Thy goodness' sake. Amen.

Samuel McComb

O Lord, Thou knowest how busy I must be
this day. If I forget Thee, do not forget me.

Sir Jacob Ashley

The day returns and brings us the petty round
of irritating concerns and duties. Help us to play the
man, help us to perform them with laughter and
kind faces, let cheerfulness abound with industry.
Give us to go blithely on our business all the day,
bring us to our resting beds weary and content and
undishonored, and grant us in the end the gift of
sleep. Amen.

Robert Louis Stevenson

O God, I cannot begin this day without Thee.
I cannot trust myself. Help me, that I may know
that I am not alone.

H. C. Alleman

For Eventide

O Lord, support us all the day long, until the shadows lengthen and the evening comes, and the busy world is hushed, and the fever of life is over, and our work is done. Then in Thy mercy grant us a safe lodging, and a holy rest, and peace at last. Amen.

John Henry Newman

Watch Thou, dear Lord, with those who wake, or watch, or weep tonight, and give Thine angels charge over those who sleep. Tend Thy sick ones, O Lord Christ, rest Thy weary ones. Bless Thy dying ones. Soothe Thy suffering ones. Pity Thy afflicted ones. Shield Thy joyous ones. And all, for Christ's sake.

St. Augustine

Night is drawing nigh. For all that has been—
Thanks! For all that shall be—Yes!

Dag Hammarskjöld

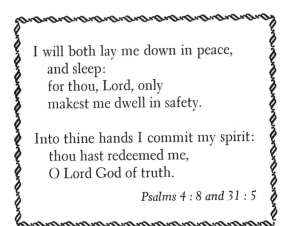

I will both lay me down in peace,
and sleep:
for thou, Lord, only
makest me dwell in safety.

Into thine hands I commit my spirit:
thou hast redeemed me,
O Lord God of truth.

Psalms 4 : 8 and 31 : 5

And now, O God, give me a quiet mind, as I lie
down to rest. Dwell in my thoughts until sleep
overtakes me. Let me not be fretted by any anxiety
over the lesser interests of life. Let no troubled
dream disturb me, so that I may awake refreshed
and ready for the tasks of another day.

John Baillie

15

Lord, receive our supplications for this house, family and country. Protect the innocent, restrain the greedy and the treacherous, lead us out of our tribulation into a quiet land.

Look down upon ourselves and our absent dear ones. Help us and them, prolong our days in peace and honor. Give us health, food, bright weather and light hearts. In what we meditate of evil, frustrate our wills; in what of good, further our endeavors. Cause injuries to be forgotten and benefits to be remembered. Let us lie down without fear and awake and arise with exultation. For His sake, in whose words we now conclude, Amen.

Robert Louis Stevenson

Into Thy hands, O God, we commend ourselves this night, and all who are dear to us. The darkness is no darkness to Thee, but the night shineth as the day. Watch over us therefore while we rest, and give us such sleep as Thou seest us to need so that in the morning we may rise refreshed and strengthened for Thy service; through Jesus Christ our Lord.

Author unknown

Lighten our darkness, we beseech thee, O Lord, and by thy great mercy defend us from all perils and dangers of this night; for the love of thy only Son, our Saviour, Jesus Christ. Amen.

The Book of Common Prayer

Send Thy peace into my heart, O Lord, that I may be contented with Thy mercies of this day and confident of Thy protection for this night; and having forgiven others, even as Thou dost forgive me, may I go to my rest in tranquillity and trust; through Jesus Christ, our Lord. Amen.

St. Francis of Assisi

Keep me this night, O Lord, from all works of darkness, and whether we wake or sleep, let our thoughts and deeds be in accordance with Thy holy will. Preserve us from all dangers and terrors of the night; from restless watching and sorrowful thoughts; from unnecessary or fretful care and imaginary fears. Let us awake tomorrow in strength, and cheerful in spirit; may we arise with holy thoughts and go forth to live to Thine honor, to the service of our fellowmen, and the comfort and joy of our households. Amen.

Gaspar Neumann

Day is done,
Gone the sun
From the lake, from the hills, from the sky.
Safely rest,
All is well!
God is nigh.

Author unknown

For Home and Family

O God,
How can I ever thank You enough
For my home?
Of all Your good ideas,
Surely this was one of the most wonderful!
O God, this tells me so much about You.
I feel that in the home
You nearly gave away Your plans—
You didn't desert me,
Like a foundling on the earth,
But left me at birth
In the loving arms of a mother.

And it is timely today to thank You
First for that home
Where I first saw the light of day.
I cannot bear to think of a life
In solitary confinement,
And I blame myself now
For not counting the blessing it was
To be cradled in affection from the first,
To be led by the hands of brothers and sisters,
And by parents who temporarily took the name of
   "Father,"
In Your place,
Until I learned from them who was.

I thank You for the home
I was given in marriage;
I tremble before the blessedness
Of being first in another's affections
Until death do us part;
For the privilege of speaking for You
To our children.
I remember the heartwarming
Homes where I was a guest,
Treated as a member of the family,
And thank You for my turn
To be host to someone else.

My mind is teeming today
With the treasures that come tumbling to me

Through the door of home:
The opportunities of teaching, learning,
Giving, receiving,
Loving, being loved;
Of dividing life into husband and wife,
The gift of companionship,
Partners to the end,
And all the wealth of comfort in our children.
Accept my thanks for all this,
For home is herald of the place
From where it came.
Teach me to live as a child here,
That I may be ready one day
To be Your child there:
How to behave to my brothers,
So I may be able to treat all Your children
As my brothers.
As I was once taught
To call my earthly parent "Father,"
Teach me how to say, "Our Father,
Who art in Heaven,"
Until You have
Your housewarming.

David A. Redding

Our families in Thine arms enfold,
As Thou didst keep Thy folk of old.

Oliver Wendell Holmes

O Lord, keep me sensitive to the grace that is
round about me. May the familiar not become
neglected! May I see Thy goodness in my daily
bread, and may the comfort of my home take my
thoughts to the mercy seat of God!

J. H. Jowett

Lord Christ, beneath Thy starry dome
We light this flickering lamp of home,
And where bewildering shadows throng
Uplift our prayer and evensong.
Dost Thou, with heaven in Thy ken
Seek still a dwelling-place with men,
Wandering the world in ceaseless quest?
O Man of Nazareth, be our guest!

Daniel Henderson

Father, this day,
For our home we pray Thee—
Our home, which, small and unknown though it be,
May yet most plainly show forth
Thine eternal glory.

May Thy love everlasting
Be reborn in our home this day;
May we take of the sacrament, all day long,
Of Thine own great love in the life of our home.

May we meet with Thee there,
May we know Thee here,
Be drawn very close to Thy side;
See revealed, in mysterious splendor,
Incarnate once more upon this earth,
Thy life, Thy love, in our home this day.

Father, we pray Thee,
Give us grace for this holiest task,
To build up a perfect home life,
That shall give to Thyself, the Omnipotent God,
Power to create, through weak human lives,
Thine own perfection of love.

J. S. Hoyland

Father, I believe that a home not built on the rock of faith hasn't a chance.

Help me to give my children a chance.

Dale Evans Rogers

For Parents

Build me a son, O Lord, who will be strong enough to know when he is weak, and brave enough to face himself when he is afraid; one who will be proud and unbending in honest defeat, and humble and gentle in victory.

Build me a son whose wishbone will not be where his backbone should be; a son who will know Thee—and that to know himself is the foundation stone of knowledge.

Lead him, I pray, not in the path of ease and comfort, but under the stress and spur of difficulties and challenge. Here, let him learn to stand up in the storm; here, let him learn compassion for those who fail.

Build me a son whose heart will be clear, whose goal will be high; a son who will master himself before he seeks to master other men; one who will learn to laugh, yet never forget how to weep; one who will reach into the future, yet never forget the past.

And after all these things are his, add, I pray, enough of a sense of humor, so that he may always be serious, yet never take himself too seriously. Give him humility, so that he may always remember the simplicity of true greatness, the open mind of true wisdom, the meekness of true strength. Then I, his father, will dare to whisper, "I have not lived in vain."

General Douglas A. MacArthur

Today, O Lord, we pray for our wayward sons and daughters. We join our prayers to the prayers of sorrowing parents, who know their children will be lost forever, if they do not repent and return to God. May we never add to their heavy burden by our undue criticism. Keep us humble and loving, O Lord. We thank Thee for the prodigals who have returned. May we ever be ready to welcome them and to forgive, as Thou art ready to forgive. We remember that we have all been prodigals.

Esther Eby Glass

For childhood's faith in us
We thank Thee, Lord.
For simple trust, expressed
By childhood's love,
Our hearts are blessed.

Grant that in fellowship
And thought refined,
We may devote our lives
To those we love,
With cheerful mind.

Let us be happy in their midst
And never disappoint them
Through any careless, flippant
Word expressed.

Help us to share their faith,
Their solid hope and trust
In every situation here
That binds us to Thy will.

We would be true to children;
We would be fair and kind and gentle.
Help all who serve to make their
Way more smooth today.

John Lewis Sandlin

✺

Lord Jesus, You who bade the children come
And took them in Your gentle arms and smiled,
Grant me unfailing patience through the days
To understand and help my little child.

I would not only give his body care
And guide his young dependent steps along
The wholesome ways, but I would know his heart,
Attuning mine to childhood's griefs and song.

Oh, give me vision to discern the child
Behind whatever he may do or say,
The wise humility to learn from him
The while I strive to teach him day by day.

Adelaide Love

Jesus, teach me how to be
Proud of my simplicity.

Sweep the floor, wash the clothes,
Gather for each vase a rose.

Iron and mend a tiny frock,
Taking notice of the clock.

Always having time kept free
For childish questions asked of me.

Grant me the wisdom Mary had
When she taught her little lad.

Catherine Cate Coblentz

 *For Youth*

O Lord Jesus, be with me all through today to help
me live as I ought to live.
Be with me at my lessons,
   so that I may never give up any task, no matter
   how hard and difficult it is, until I have
   mastered it, and so that I will not allow
   anything to beat me.
Be with me at my games,
   so that, whether I win or lose, I may play fair,
   and so that if I win I may not boast, and if I
   lose, I may not make excuses.
Be with me in my pleasure,
   so that I may never find pleasure in anything
   that I would afterward regret, or in anything
   that I would not like you or my parents to see
   me do.

Be with me in my home,
>	so that I may be kind and considerate, and
>	that I may try to make the work of others
>	easier and not harder.

Be with me in the streets,
>	so that I may be a credit to my school and to
>	those who love me and to myself.

Help me to be the kind of person you want me to
be.

This I ask for your love's sake.

William Barclay

Lord, for these simple things I plead:

That my mind may be a quiet harbor where ships of
thought may dock;

That my heart may be a temple of love;

That my soul be a flourishing vine that reaches
steadily upward toward heaven and God;

That my religion be as a loaf of bread that gives
nourishment to me and my hungering neighbor.

That my life may be a light kept aglow by the fuel
of kindly deeds done for others;

That my friendship be a cool, bubbling brook where
all races may drink its water;

Lastly, that I be dedicated to the truth and clothed
in the fire of righteousness.

Wilma Curtis

O God, sometimes I am tempted
because cheating seems to be the easiest
and quickest way to get what I want.
Forgive me for the times
I have told lies, kept miscounted change,
or misled my friends. Grant that I shall come to
love truth and hate lies—especially my own. May all
my words and deeds be free of sham and
    make-believe.

In the classroom, in games
with my friends, as I trade at the store, help me
to be completely trustworthy.

Day by day may I live
in such close friendship with Thee that there will be
nothing in my life
which is counterfeit or insincere. Amen.

Walter L. Cook

    Help us, O Lord, to find the standards for
accomplishing fellowship in this life. Teach us how
to practice the spirit of understanding and goodwill.
May we share the fellowship of Christ. Amen.

John Lewis Sandlin

Let no unworthy thought
Enter thy musing mind;
Things which the world hath wrought,
Untrue, unclean, unkind,
Leave these behind.

Toc-H prayer

O God, give each of us the will and strength to
use the facts, the principles, and the values that we
have learned as we respond to the challenges and
the problems that we shall confront.

Help us to accept what we must accept, but to
know when it is time for us to rebel. Help us to
know when to compromise and when to refuse to
compromise, to know when to doubt and when
to trust.

Help us to broaden our perspective without
abandoning our beliefs, to deepen our sensitivity,
and to increase our concern for our fellowman. Help
us to convert our thought into action, and to
understand the significance of what we do. Above
all, help us to love. Amen.

Arminal Elizabeth Hay

Dear Lord, here at the beginning of my life, I want desperately to know two things: who I am, and what you would have me to do with my one life. I must know, soon. Could you let me know, Lord?

Author unknown

There is no use
Giving a snow job to you, Lord.
You already know me like a book.

So when I'm all alone
Help me to see me like I am
Even if I don't like it.

Inside of me I want the right thing,
Then when I'm with someone
I want them to think I'm the big man.

When I'm all alone tonight, God,
Help me see
What you want me to be like.

Carl F. Burke

 *For Any and Every Day*

Give me, amidst the confusion of my day,
    the calmness of the everlasting hills.
Break the tension of my nerves and muscles
    with the soothing music of the singing streams
        that live in my memory.
            Help me to know
            the magical restorative power of sleep.
Teach me the art of taking minute vacations . . .
    of slowing down to look at a flower,
        to chat with a friend,
            to pat a dog,
    to read a few lines from a good book.
        Slow me down, Lord,
    and inspire me to send my roots deep
    into the soil of life's enduring values,
        that I may grow
    toward the stars of my greater destiny.

W. E. *Sangster*

Give us grace, O Lord, to work while it is day, fulfilling diligently and patiently whatever duty Thou appointest us; doing small things in the day of small things, and great labours if Thou summonest us to any; rising and working, sitting still and suffering according to Thy word.

Christina Georgina Rossetti

There is no place
Where God is not.
Wherever I go, there God is.
Now and always He upholds
Me with His power.
And keeps me safe in
His love.

Author unknown

Lord of all pots and pans and things, since I've no time to be
A saint doing lovely things or watching late with Thee,

Or dreaming in the dawnlight or storming heaven's
    gates,
Make me a saint by getting meals and washing up
    the plates.

Although I must have Martha's hands, I have a
    Mary mind;
And as I black the boots and shoes, Thy sandals,
    Lord, I find.
I think of how they trod the earth; what time I
    scrub the floor,
Accept this meditation, Lord; I haven't time for
    more.

Warm all the kitchen with Thy love, and light it
    with Thy peace;
Forgive me all my worryings, and make all
    grumblings cease.
Thou who didst love to give men food, in room or
    by the sea,
Accept this service that I do—I do it unto Thee.

Cecily Hallack

Grant me, I beseech Thee, O merciful God,
prudently to study, rightly to understand, and
perfectly to fulfill that which is pleasing to Thee, to
the praise and glory of Thy name. Amen.

St. Thomas Aquinas

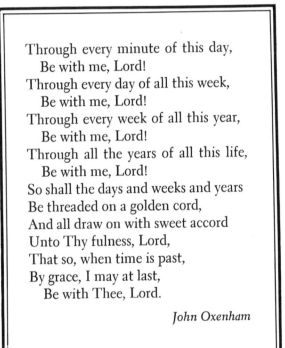

Through every minute of this day,
   Be with me, Lord!
Through every day of all this week,
   Be with me, Lord!
Through every week of all this year,
   Be with me, Lord!
Through all the years of all this life,
   Be with me, Lord!
So shall the days and weeks and years
Be threaded on a golden cord,
And all draw on with sweet accord
Unto Thy fulness, Lord,
That so, when time is past,
By grace, I may at last,
   Be with Thee, Lord.

John Oxenham

Let me do my work each day; and if the darkened hours of despair overcome me, may I not forget the strength that comforted me in the desolation of other times.

May I still remember the bright hours that found me walking over the silent hills of my childhood, or dreaming, on the margin of the quiet river, when a light glowed within me, and I promised my early God to have courage amid the tempests of the changing years. Spare me from bitterness and from the sharp passions of unguarded moments. May I not forget that poverty and riches are of the spirit. Though the world know me not, may my thoughts and actions be such as shall keep me friendly with myself.

Lift my eyes from the earth, and let me not forget the uses of the stars. Forbid that I should judge others lest I condemn myself. Let me not follow the clamor of the world, but walk calmly in my path.

Give me a few friends who will love me for what I am; and keep ever burning before my vagrant steps the kindly light of hope. And though age and infirmity overtake me, and I come not within sight of the castle of my dreams, teach me still to be thankful for life and for time's olden memories that are good and sweet, and may the evening's twilight find me gentle still.

Max Ehrmann

Loving Jesu, gentle Lamb,
In Thy gracious hands I am;
Make me, Saviour, what Thou art!
Live Thyself within my heart.

I shall then show forth Thy praise;
Serve Thee all my happy days;
Then the world shall always see
Christ, the Holy Child, in me.

Charles Wesley

 *For All Things Bright and Good*

We thank Thee, now, O Father,
  For all things bright and good,
The seedtime and the harvest,
  Our life, our health, our food;
Accept the gifts we offer
  For all Thy love imparts,
And, what Thou most desirest,
  Our humble, thankful hearts.

Matthius Claudius

O most high, Almighty, good Lord God, to Thee belong praise, glory, honor, and all blessing!

Praised be my Lord God for all His creatures, especially for our brother the sun, who brings us the day and who brings us the light; fair is he and shineth with a very great splendor: O Lord, he signifies to us Thee!

Praised be my Lord for our sister the moon, and for the stars, the which He has set clear and lovely in heaven.

Praised be my Lord for our brother the wind, and for air and clouds, calms and all weather, by the which Thou upholdest life in all creatures.

Praised be my Lord for our sister water, who is very serviceable unto us and humble and precious and clean.

Praised be my Lord for our brother fire, through whom Thou givest us light in darkness; and he is bright and pleasant and very mighty and strong.

Praised be my Lord for our mother the earth, the which doth sustain us and keep us and bring forth divers fruits and flowers of many colors, and grass.

Praised be my Lord for all those who pardon one another for His love's sake, and who endure weakness and tribulation: blessed are they who peaceably shall endure, for Thou, O Most Highest, shalt give them a crown.

Praised be my Lord for our sister the death of
the body, from which no man escapeth. Woe to
him who dies in mortal sin! Blessed are they who
are found walking by Thy holy will, for the second
death shall have no power to do them harm.

Praise ye and bless the Lord, and give thanks
unto Him, and serve Him with great humility.
Amen.

St. Francis of Assisi

I see Thee in the distant blue;
But in the violet's dell of dew,
Behold, I breathe and touch Thee too.

John Banister Tabb

O God, we thank Thee for everything.
For the sea and its waves, blue, green and gray and
    always wonderful;
For the beach and for the breakers and the spray
    and the white foam on the rocks;
For the blue arch of heaven; for the clouds in the
    sky, white and gray and purple;
For the green of the grass; for the forests in their
    spring beauty; for the wheat and corn and rye and
    barley.

We thank Thee for all Thou hast made and that
    Thou hast called it good;
For all the glory and beauty and wonder of the
    world.
We thank Thee that Thou hast placed us in the
    world to subdue all things to Thy glory,
And to use all things for the good of Thy children.

Edward Everett Hale

 *For Others*

O God, make me discontent with things the way
    they are in the world,
    and in my life.
Teach me how to blush again,
    for the tawdry deals,
    the arrogant-but-courteous prejudice,
    the snickers,
    the leers,
    the good food and drink which makes me too
      weary to repent,
    the flattery given and received,

my willing use of rights and privileges other
    men are unfairly denied.
Make me notice the stains when people get spilled
on.
Make me care about the slum child downtown,
    the misfit at work,
    the people crammed into the mental hospital,
    the men, women, and youth behind bars.
Jar my complacence; expose my excuses; get me
    involved in the life of my community,
    and give me integrity once more.

Robert Raines

Lord Jesus, bless all who serve us, who have
dedicated their lives to the ministry of others—all
the teachers in our schools who labor so patiently
with so little appreciation; all who wait upon the
public, the clerks in the stores who have to accept
criticism, complaints, bad manners, selfishness, at
the hands of a thoughtless public. Bless the
mailmen, the drivers of streetcars and buses who
must listen to people who have lost their tempers.

    Bless every humble soul who, in these days of
stress and strain, preaches sermons without words.

Peter Marshall

May the road rise to meet you,
May the wind be always at your back . . .
And may God hold you
In the palm of His hand.

Old Gaelic prayer

Grant, O Lord, that in all the joys of life we may never forget to be kind. Help us to be unselfish in friendship, thoughtful of those less happy than ourselves, and eager to bear the burdens of others.

Charles L. Slattery

Lord, help me live from day to day
In such a self-forgetful way,
That even when I kneel to pray,
My prayer may be for—*others*.

Charles Dickens

All through this day, O Lord, by the power of Thy quickening Spirit, let me touch the lives of others for good, whether through the word I speak, the prayer I speak, or the life I live.

Author unknown

Father, accept this prayer of apology for something we did not do in church this morning. A strange old lady came to worship with us, and nobody but the pastor and an usher spoke to her. She went away looking so lonely and unhappy, and she will not come to us again. We were all so busy with the business of the church that we forgot what our Father's business is, and we are ashamed.

Can you forgive us once again, and help us to think more of others and less of ourselves, when we pray, and before and after prayer? We are grateful for Thy patience, Lord. Amen.

George H. Spencer

They wouldn't even answer the door.
I knocked a dozen times, Lord, and heard their
    raucous laugh muffle into stark silence.
All I needed was a telephone. Why didn't they open
    up?
Between slats in the blinds I could see people at a
    card table. They were four, and I was one.
In sheets of rain it was my fifth attempt at a lighted
    house, but nobody answers doors anymore after
    dark. No telling how far a garage was, and the
    car konked out two blocks back.

I pounded harder, trying to shake water from my
   clothes.
  "Go away," a voice called.
  "I need help!"
  "He doesn't live here."
  "Could you call a garage for me?"
Silence. Then through a locked door,
  "It'll be twenty minutes."

Lord, do you know how hard it is to find a
  Samaritan?

Jeanette Struchen

Dear Lord! Kind Lord!
 Gracious Lord! I pray
Thou will look on all I love
 Tenderly today.
Weed their hearts of weariness;
 Scatter every care
Down a wake of angel-wings
 Winnowing the air.

Bring unto the sorrowing
 All release from pain;
Let the lips of laughter
 Overflow again;

44

And with all the needy,
    O divide, I pray,
This vast measure of content
    That is mine today!

James Whitcomb Riley

For God and Country

This is my song, O God of all nations,
A song of peace for lands afar, and mine.
This is my hope, the country where my heart is.
This is my hope, my dream, and my shrine.
But other hearts in other lands are beating
With hopes and dreams that are the same as mine.

My country's skies are bluer than the ocean,
The sunlight beams on clover leaf and pine;
But other lands have sunlight too, and clover,
And other skies are just as blue as mine.
O hear my prayer, Thou God of all the nations,
A prayer of peace for other lands and mine.

Author unknown

O God, the Father of all men,
>   Thou who governest the nations upon the
>   earth,
>   look with mercy upon us and hear our prayer.
Remember not the offenses of Thy people,
>   our many transgressions and our mighty sin.
Have mercy upon us.

Save us as men and nations from the pride of
>   possessions,
>   from boastings and from national hypocrisies.
Save Thy people, O Lord, from hard bargainings,
>   from service to things
>   and from worship of wealth and power.

Hear our prayer, O Lord, that we may make
>   the wise choice of those who are to govern us;
>   and just legislators,
>   faithful judges and representatives,
>   and may Thy godly spirit guide us as a people
>   in our choice of those who govern our land
>   in its relation to other nations.
We lift our voices and hearts in prayer,
>   especially for the President of the United States
>   and those who share his responsibilities.
May they be granted abundant grace, pure motives
>   and right judgment,
And may the councils of the nations

know of Thy power and Thy justice
and seek to do His will,
Which is peace among Thy children.

Cleanse us from all that defiles our national life:
from indifference and idolatry,
from prejudice and pride,
and self-satisfaction and smugness,
from selfishness and sophistication,
from profaneness and intemperance.

Cleanse us, O Lord, for only those with clean hands
and a pure heart may see Thee.
"Except the Lord build the house,
they labor in vain that build it. . . ."
In His name we pray this prayer, "*Our Father. . . .*"

Herman N. Beimfohr

✿

Almighty God, the time has passed for long
speeches. The time has passed for rich, full oratory.
Please, dear God, help us to get at the heart of the
matter—and help us to get there fast.

*The Reverend Donald J. Curran, at the
New York State Constitutional
Convention*

47

Lord, though I am a miserable and wretched creature, I am in Covenant with Thee through grace. And I may, I will, come to Thee, for Thy people. Thou hast made me, though very unworthy, a mean instrument to do them some good, and Thee service; and many of them have set too high a value upon me, though others wish and would be glad of my death; Lord, however Thou dost dispose of me, continue and go on to do good for them. Give them consistency of judgment, one heart, and mutual love; and go on to deliver them, and with the work of reformation; and make the name of Christ glorious to the world. Teach those who look too much on Thy instruments, to depend more upon Thyself. Pardon such as desire to trample upon the dust of a poor worm, for they are Thy people too. And pardon the folly of this short Prayer:—even for Jesus Christ's sake. And give me a good night, if it be Thy pleasure. Amen.

Oliver Cromwell

Where the mind is without fear and the head is
    held high;
Where knowledge is free;
Where the world has not been broken up into
    fragments by narrow domestic walls;

Where words come out from the depth of truth;
Where tireless striving stretches its arms toward
 perfection;
Where the clear stream of reason has not lost its
 way unto the dreary desert sand of dead habit;
Where the mind is led forward in the ever-widening
 thought and action—
Into that heaven of freedom, my Father, let my
 country awake.

Rabindranath Tagore

Help us, our Father, to show other nations an America to imitate—not the America of loud jazz music, self-seeking indulgence, and love of money, but the America that loves fair play, honest dealing, straight talk, real freedom, and faith in God.

Make us see that it cannot be done as long as we are content to be coupon clippers on the original investment made by our forefathers.

Give us faith in God and love for our fellowmen, that we may have something to deposit on which the young people of today can draw interest tomorrow.

By Thy grace, let this day increase the moral capital of this country. Amen.

Peter Marshall

God send us men whose aim 'twill be,
Not to defend some outworn creed,
But to live out the laws of Christ
In every thought and deed.
God send us men alert and quick
His lofty precepts to translate,
Until the laws of Christ become
The laws and habits of the state.

Frederick J. Gillman

For Those Who Would Serve

Lord, make me an instrument of Thy peace.
Where there is hatred, let me sow love;
Where there is injury, pardon;
Where there is doubt, faith;
Where there is despair, hope;
Where there is darkness, light;
Where there is sadness, joy.

O Divine Master, grant that
I may not so much seek

To be consoled, as to console;
Not so much to be understood as
To understand; not so much to be
Loved as to love;
For it is in giving that we receive;
It is in pardoning that we are pardoned;
It is in dying that we awaken to eternal life.

St. Francis of Assisi

Govern all by Thy wisdom, O Lord, so that my soul may be serving Thee as Thou dost will, and not as I may choose. Do not punish me, I beseech Thee, by granting that which I wish or ask, if it offend Thy love, which would always live in me. Let me die to myself, that I may serve Thee, who in Thyself art the true life. Amen.

St. Teresa of Avila

If indeed it be necessary, O Lord, to bury the workman that my work may be finished by other hands, help me never to think of myself as indispensable. May I be content to die with my work undone, knowing that my task is to work at the fulfillment of Thy purposes, not to work them out.

Author unknown

Oh, God, Thou puttest into my heart this great desire to devote myself to the sick and sorrowful; I offer it to Thee. Do with it what is for Thy service.

Oh, my Creator, art Thou leading every man of us to perfection? Or is this only a metaphysical idea for which there is no evidence? Is man only a constant repetition of himself? Thou knowest that through all these twenty horrible years I have been supported by the belief (I think I must believe it still or I am sure I could not work) that I was working with Thee Who wert bringing every one of us, even our poor nurses, to perfection. O Lord, even now I am trying to snatch the management of Thy world from Thy hands. Too little have I looked for something higher and better than my own work —the work of supreme Wisdom, which uses us whether we know it or not.

Florence Nightingale

Use me, then, my Saviour, for whatever purpose, and in whatever way, Thou mayest require. Here is my poor heart, an empty vessel; fill it with Thy grace. Here is my sinful and troubled soul; quicken it and refresh it with Thy love. Take mine heart for Thine abode; my mouth to spread abroad the glory of Thy name; my love and all my powers, for the advancement of Thy believing people; and never suffer the steadfastness and confidence of my faith to abate; —so that at all times I may be enabled from the heart to say, "Jesus needs me, and I am His."

Dwight L. Moody

O God, set our hearts at liberty from the service of ourselves, and let it be our meat and drink to do Thy will.

Henry S. Nash

O God,
Help us to be masters of ourselves,
That we may become the servants of others.

Alec Paterson

Lord, take my lips, and speak through them; take my mind, and think through it; take my heart, and set it on fire. Amen.

W. H. Aitken

 *For Those Who Need Help*

Nothing can frighten me, O my Jesus, neither rain nor wind; and if the dark clouds descend to hide Thee from my sight, I shall not move, knowing that above the clouds the sunshine of Thy love shines forever, and that its splendor can not be eclipsed for a single moment!

O Lord, Thou wouldst not inspire me with unattainable desires! Therefore, in spite of my smallness, I shall aspire to sanctity. It is impossible, O Jesus, to make me great! Therefore I must bear with myself as I am, with all my imperfections. Yet I shall look for a means of going to heaven by a little path that is very straight and very, very short, a path that is entirely new.

We are in a century of inventions: it is no longer necessary to climb the steps of a stairway, for in the houses of the rich an elevator has replaced them comfortably! And I want to find an elevator that will lift me up to Thee, Jesus, for I am too little a creature to climb the bitter stairway of perfection. . . . The elevator that must raise me to heaven is Your arms, O my Jesus! Therefore I do not need to grow in size—in fact I must remain little and strive to become smaller still!

St. Teresa of Lisieux

O Lord, my God! The amazing horrors of darkness were gathered round me, and covered me all over, and I saw no way to go forth; I felt the depth and extent of the misery of my fellow creatures separated from the divine harmony, and it was heavier than I could bear; and I was crushed down under it; I lifted up my hand, I stretched out my arm, but there was none to help me; I looked round about, and was amazed. In the depths of misery, O Lord, I remembered that Thou art omnipotent; that I had called Thee Father; and I felt that I loved Thee, and I was made quiet in my will, and I waited for deliverance from Thee. Thou hadst pity on me, when no man could help me; I saw that meekness under suffering was showed to us in the most affecting example of Thy Son, and Thou taughtest me to follow Him, and I said, "Thy will, O Father, be done!"

John Woolman

Lord Jesus Christ, who alone art wisdom, Thou knowest what is best for us; mercifully grant that it may happen to us only as it is pleasing to Thee and as seems good in Thy sight this day, for Thy name's sake. Amen.

Henry VI of England

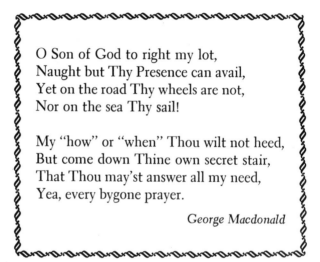

O Son of God to right my lot,
Naught but Thy Presence can avail,
Yet on the road Thy wheels are not,
Nor on the sea Thy sail!

My "how" or "when" Thou wilt not heed,
But come down Thine own secret stair,
That Thou may'st answer all my need,
Yea, every bygone prayer.

George Macdonald

Speak to me low, my Saviour,
From out the hallelujahs, sweet and low,
Lest I should fear and fall, and miss Thee so
Who art not missed by any that entreat.

Speak to me as to Mary at Thy feet—
And if no precious gums my hands bestow,
Let my tears drop like amber, while I go
In reach of Thy divinest voice complete
In humanest affection—thus, in sooth,
To lose the sense of losing! As a child,
Whose song-bird seeks the wood for evermore,
Is sung to in its stead by mother's mouth;
Till, sinking on her breast, love-reconciled,
He sleeps the faster that he wept before.

Elizabeth Barrett Browning

Lead us in the way wherein we should walk, O
God, and quicken us to do Thy will; for Thou art
our Father, we are Thy children, and we need the
touch of Thy hand.

Frederica Beard

Grant me, O Lord, to know what I ought to
know, to love what I ought to love, to praise what
delights Thee most, to value what is precious in Thy
sight, and to hate what is offensive to Thee.

Thomas à Kempis

Behold, Lord, an empty vessel that needs to be filled. My Lord, fill it. I am weak in the faith; strengthen Thou me. I am cold in love; warm me and make me fervent that my love may go out to my neighbor. I do not have a strong and firm faith; at times I doubt and am unable to trust Thee altogether. O Lord, help me. Strengthen my faith and trust in Thee. In Thee I have sealed the treasure of all I have. I am poor; Thou art rich and didst come to be merciful to the poor. I am a sinner; Thou art upright. With me, there is an abundance of sin, in Thee is the fullness of righteousness. Therefore I will remain with Thee of whom I can receive, but to whom I may not give. Amen.

Martin Luther

Our Father, give us the faith to believe that it is possible for us to live victoriously even in the midst of dangerous opportunity that we call crisis. Help us to see that there is something better than patient endurance or keeping a stiff upper lip, and that whistling in the dark is not really bravery.

Trusting in Thee, may we have the faith that goes singing in the rain, knowing that all things work together for good to them that love Thee. Through Jesus Christ our Lord. Amen.

Peter Marshall

Lord, without Thee I can do nothing; with Thee I can do all. Help me by Thy grace, that I fall not; help me by Thy strength to resist nightly the very first beginnings of evil, before it takes hold of me; help me to cast myself at once at Thy sacred feet, and lie still there, until the storm be overpast; and, if I lose sight of Thee, bring me quickly back to Thee, and grant me to love Thee better.

E. B. Pusey

O Lord, our only Saviour, we cannot bear alone our load of responsibility: upbear us under it.

We look without seeing unless Thou purge our sight: grant us sight.

We read without comprehending unless Thou open our understanding: give us intelligence.

Nothing can we do unless Thou prosper the work of our hands upon us: oh, prosper Thou our handiwork.

We are weak: out of weakness make us strong. We are in peril of death: come and heal us. We believe: help Thou our unbelief. We hope: let us not be disappointed of our hope. We love: grant us to love much, to love ever more and more, to love all, and most of all to love Thee.

Christina Georgina Rossetti

O Lord God, grant us always, whatever the world may say, to content ourselves with what Thou wilt say, and to care only for Thy approval, which will outweigh all worlds; for Jesus Christ's sake.

Charles George Gordon

It's me, it's me, it's me, O Lord,
Standin' in the need of prayer.
Not my brother, not my sister,
But it's me, O Lord,
Standin' in the need of prayer.

Negro spiritual

If I have faltered more or less
In my great task of happiness;
If I have moved among my race
And shown no shining morning face;
If beams from happy human eyes
Have moved me not; if morning skies,
Books, and my food, and summer rain,
Knocked on my sullen heart in vain:
Lord, Thy most pointed pleasure take
And stab my spirit broad awake.

Robert Louis Stevenson

Lord, I am like to mistletoe,
Which has no root and cannot grow
Or prosper, but by the same tree
It clings about: so I by Thee.
What need I then to fear at all
So long as I about Thee crawl?
But if that tree should fall and die,
Tumble shall heaven, and so will I.

Robert Herrick

For Those Who Need Forgiveness

Forgive all of us who feel no thankfulness.
Forgive those of us who stroll into life
    and stroll out
      as though its gifts had always been there
      and cost nothing.
Forgive those who find life and spend it
    like spending a coin
    caring not who earned it.
O God, forgive our many sins of ingratitude.

Herman N. Beimfohr

Dear Lord and Father of mankind,
　　Forgive our foolish ways!
Reclothe us in our rightful mind;
In purer lives Thy service find,
　　In deeper reverence, praise.

John Greenleaf Whittier

O Lord, forgive what I have been, sanctify what I am, and order what I shall be.

Anonymous

Our Father, Who art in heaven, we are Thy children on this earth. Rich and poor, black and white, Jew and Gentile, native and alien, friend and enemy—we are all alike the heirs of Thy providence and the recipients of Thy love. As Thou hast done for us, so we should do for one another. But we have been selfish and cruel, and unrighteously have sought to serve not Thy will but our own.

We confess before Thee, O God, the sins of which we have been guilty. We have corrupted government, exploited labor, oppressed women and little children, played upon the weak and helpless, ground the faces of the poor, done public injustice for private gain. These are our hands, stained with the evil of our deeds! Behold our hearts, impure with sordid desires for place and profit! The world, which Thou hast made so fair, we have defaced. Our country, which Thou hast so richly blessed, we have defamed. Woe be unto us, that wickedness has so prevailed among us.

But Thou art patient, O God, and strong to save. Thy righteousness is mighty upon us, and cannot fail. Thou art building Thy kingdom in the hearts of men as from the beginning of the world, and seeking our aid as fellow-laborers with Thee. So would we turn to Thee, to plead Thy forgiveness as we cleanse the dark places of our lust and pride.

Help us to strive to do justice, to love mercy, and to walk humbly with Thee in the way of righteousness. We would rid this nation's life of its abominations. Throughout the world we would deliver men from inequality, indignity, and oppression. We would end poverty and war, establish freedom and security, and drive fear from every heart. We would reward the labor of men's hands with prosperity, and the love of men's souls with peace. So would we bring in that common-wealth of man which shall be Thy kingdom come at last upon the earth. In Thy name and for Thy sake, we ask it. Amen.

John Haynes Holmes

For you are the Lord Most High,
Tender-hearted, long-suffering, and most merciful,
And regretful of the wickedness of men.
You have ordained repentance for a sinner like me,
For my sins more numerous than the sands of the
    sea.
Now therefore I bend the knee of my heart, begging
    you for kindness.
Forgive me, Lord, forgive me!
For you, Lord, are the God of those who repent,
And you will manifest your goodness toward me,
For, unworthy as I am, you will save me in the
    abundance of your mercy,
And I will praise you continually as long as I live.
And yours is the glory forever. Amen.

Prayer of Manasseh, in the Apocrypha

Forgive us, if you can, dear Lord,
    the sin of the closed mind;
    our effrontery in trying to play God;
    for asking so much of you and
        giving so little of ourselves;
    our begging for miracles when we
        could do it ourselves;
    for dragging our feet in kingdom-building,
    for wanting Thy crowns without Thy crosses.

Author unknown

O Lord, forgive us for being so sensitive about the things that do not matter, and so insensitive to the things that do.

Roy L. Smith

Almighty and most merciful Father; We have erred, and strayed from thy ways like lost sheep. We have followed too much the devices and desires of our own hearts. We have offended against thy holy laws. We have left undone those things which we ought to have done; And we have done those things which we ought not to have done; And there is no health in us. But thou, O Lord, have mercy upon us, miserable offenders. Spare thou those, O God, who confess thy faults. Restore thou those who are penitent; According to thy promises declared unto mankind In Christ Jesus our Lord. And grant, O most merciful Father, for his sake; That we may hereafter live a godly, righteous, and sober life, To the glory of thy holy Name. Amen.

The Book of Common Prayer

For Those Who Would Ask God for Something

Jesus, He loves us one and all,
Jesus, He loves children small,
Their souls are waiting round His feet,
On high, before His mercy-seat.

While He wandered here below,
Children small to Him did go.
At His feet they knelt and prayed,
On their heads His hands He laid.

Came a Spirit on them then,
Better than of mighty men,
A Spirit faithful, pure, and mild,
A Spirit fit for king or child.

Oh! that spirit give to me,
Jesus, Lord, where'er I be!

Charles Kingsley

Thou hast called us to Thyself, most merciful father, with love and with promises abundant; and we are witnesses that it is not in vain that we draw near to Thee. We bear witness to Thy faithfulness. Thy promises are Yea and Amen. Thy blessings are exceeding abundant, more than we know or think. We thank Thee for the privilege of prayer, and for Thine answer according to our petitions. We are blind, and constantly seeking things which are not best for us. If Thou didst grant all our desires according to our requests, we should be ruined. In dealing with our little children we give them, not the things which they ask for, but the things which we judge to be best for them; and Thou, our Father, art by Thy providence overruling our ignorance and our headlong mistakes, and are doing for us, not so much the things that we request of Thee as the things that we should ask; and we are, day by day, saved from peril and from ruin by Thy better knowledge and by Thy careful love. Amen.

Henry Ward Beecher

O God, mercifully grant unto us that the fire of Thy love may burn up in us all things that displease Thee, and make us meet for Thy heavenly kingdom.

Roman breviary

Grant me, O Lord, to know what I ought to know,
to love what I ought to love,
to praise what delights Thee most,
to value what is precious in Thy sight,
to hate what is offensive to Thee.
Do not suffer me to judge according to the sight of
my eyes,
nor to pass sentence according to the hearing of the
ears of ignorant men;
but to discern with a true judgment between things
visible and spiritual,
and above all, always to inquire what is the good
pleasure of Thy will.

Thomas à Kempis

Help us, in our work and in our play, to be
physically strong, mentally awake, and morally
straight. All of which we ask in the name of the
Great Friend and Master of men. Amen.

West Point cadet prayer

What we need to know teach Thou us; what we
cannot know make us content to leave unknown,
and to wait patiently on Thee till the shadows flee
away.

John Hunter

Give ear, O Lord, unto our prayer, and attend to the voice of our supplication.

Make us poor in spirit: that ours may be the kingdom of heaven.

Make us to mourn for sin: that we may be comforted by Thy grace.

Make us meek: that we may inherit the earth.

Make us to hunger and thirst after righteousness: that we may be filled therewith.

Make us merciful: that we may obtain mercy.

Make us pure in heart: that we may see Thee.

Make us peacemakers: that we may be called thy children.

Make us willing to be persecuted for righteousness' sake: that our reward may be great in heaven.

The Book of Common Order

O God, grant us the serenity to accept what cannot be changed, the courage to change what can be changed, and the wisdom to know the one from the other.

Reinhold Niebuhr

God open my eyes
    that I may see
And feel Your presence
    close to me. . . .
Give me strength
    for my stumbling feet
As I battle the crowd
    on life's busy street,
And widen the vision
    of my unseeing eyes
So in passing faces
    I'll recognize
Not just a stranger,
    unloved and unknown,
But a friend with a heart
    that is much like my own. . . .
Give me perception
    to make me aware
That scattered profusely
    on life's thoroughfare
Are the best gifts of God
    that we daily pass by
As we look at the world
    with an unseeing eye.

Helen Steiner Rice

Give us, Lord, a bit o' sun—
A bit o' work, a bit o' fun;
Give us air in th' struggle and splutter;
Our daily bread, an' a bit o' butter!
Give us health, our keep to make,
An' a bit to spare for poor folks' sake;
Give us sense, for we're some o' us duffers;
An' a heart to feel for aw' that suffers;
Give us, too, a bit of song,
An' a tale, an' a book, to help us along;
An' give us our share o' sorrow's lesson,
That we may prove how grief's blessin'.
Give us, Lord, a chance to be
Our gradely best, brave, wise, an' free,
Our gradely best for ourselves an' others
Till aw' men larn to live as brothers.

From a Lancaster country inn

Drop Thy still dews of quietness,
   Till all our strivings cease;
Take from our souls the strain and stress,
   And let our ordered lives confess
   The beauty of Thy peace.

John Greenleaf Whittier

71

 *For Those Who Would
Thank God for Something*

There's not a plant or flower below,
But makes Thy glories known;
And clouds arise, and tempests blow,
By order from Thy throne,
While all that borrows life from Thee
Is ever in Thy care,
And everywhere that man can be,
Thou, God, art present there.

Isaac Watts

I thank Thee, Lord, for all the little things
    That are so great a part of every day—
The dawn, the dusk, the high bright sun at noon,
    And the glad voice of children at their play.

72

I thank Thee for the house in which I live,
  For the gray roof on which the raindrops slant;
I thank Thee for a garden and the slim young shoots
  That mark old-fashioned things I plant.

I thank Thee for a daily task to do,
  For books that are my ships with golden wings,
For mighty gifts let others offer praise—
  Lord, I am thanking Thee for little things.

Author unknown

It's a glorious feeling to be able
        to unload my heart,
        to spill out my gratitude
        in thanks to You, O God.
Morning, noon, and night
        I want the whole world to know of Your love.
I want to shout it, sing it,
        in every possible way
        to proclaim Your praises,
        to express my joy.
How great You are, O Lord!
Your thoughts are unfathomable,
Your ways beyond comprehension.

And all the while we are still confounded
     over the problem of evil.
We simply cannot understand
     why the ungodly appear to be so successful,
     why good fortune seems to follow those
     who defy You.
But we know their success is short lived.
Those who refuse to turn to You will never find
     that ultimate and total fulfillment
     that is promised to the sons of God.
The children of God,
     those who open their lives to You,
     portray the wonder and beauty of Your Spirit.
They are like springs of water in a parched world.
They flourish even amid the distortions
     and the ugliness around them,
Their lives are rich and productive
     in a barren and desolate society.
Help us, those of us who love You, O God,
     to prove to our disjointed world
     that You are in our midst.

Paraphrase of the prayer in
Psalm 92, by Leslie F. Brandt

God—there are things in my life I don't like,
     Folks I can't bear.
But there are more things I would hate to change,
     Friends I can't spare.

So when You hear me complaining aloud,
    Just turn away;
Deep inside my ungracious heart, I am
    Grateful each day.
Amen.

Author unknown

Thank You very much indeed—

Spring, for wood anemones
    near the mossy toes of trees;
Summer, for the fruited pear,
    yellowing crab, and cherry fare;
Autumn, for the bearded load,
    hazelnuts along the road;
Winter, for the fairy tale,
    spitting log, and bouncing hail.

But, blest Father, high above,
    all these joys are from Thy love;
And your children everywhere,
    born in palace, lane or square,
Cry with voices all agreed,
    "Thank You very much indeed."

Norman Gale

I thank Thee, Lord, for mine unanswered prayers,
    Unanswered, save Thy quiet, kindly "Nay."
Yet it seemed hard among my heavy cares
    That bitter day.

I wanted joy: but Thou didst know for me
    That sorrow was the lift I needed most,
And in its mystic depths I learned to see
    The Holy Ghost.

I wanted health; but Thou didst bid me sound
    The secret treasuries of pain,
And in the moans and groans my heart oft found
    Thy Christ again.

I wanted wealth; 'twas not the better part;
    There is a wealth of poverty oft given,
And Thou didst teach me of the gold of heart,
    Best gift of heaven.

I thank Thee, Lord, for these unanswered prayers,
    And for Thy word, the quiet, kindly "Nay."
'Twas Thy withholding lightened all my cares
    That blessed day.

Author unknown

Thank God for dirty dishes;
They have a story to tell.
And by the stack I have
It seems we are living very well.
While people of other countries are starving
I haven't the heart to fuss,
For by this stack of evidence
God's awfully good to us.

A high-school girl

For Those Who Go to Church

On entering the church:

"Almighty God, unto whom all hearts are open,
all desires known, and from whom no secrets are
hid: Cleanse the thoughts of our hearts by the
inspiration of thy Holy Spirit, that we may perfectly
love thee, and worthily magnify thy holy Name;
through Christ our Lord. Amen."

Book of Common Prayer

On leaving the church:

"Our Father, we have listened to Thy word, and loved it; we have found comfort and inspiration in song and psalter; we have enjoyed the companionship of those who, with kindred minds and hearts, have praised and worshiped Thee. Now help us to understand that, as we leave this sacred House of God, we shall become Thy Church in the street."

Author unknown

For Two Very Special Days

Loving Father, help us remember the birth of Jesus, that we may share in the song of the angels, the gladness of the shepherds, and the wisdom of the wise men.

Close the door of hate and open the door of love all over the world.

Let kindness come with every gift and good desires with every greeting.

Deliver us from evil by the blessing which
Christ brings, and teach us to be merry with clean
hearts.

May the Christmas morning make us happy to
be Thy children, and the Christmas evening bring
us to our beds with grateful thoughts, forgiving and
forgiven, for Jesus' sake. Amen.

Robert Louis Stevenson

O Lord, there sit apart in lonely places,
  On this, the gladdest night of all the year,
Some stricken ones, with sad and weary faces
    To whom the thought of Christmas brings no
      cheer;
For these, O Father, our petition hear,
  And send the pitying Christ Child very near.

Author unknown

Because in tender majesty
Thou cam'st to earth, nor stayed till we,
Poor sinners, stumbled up to Thee,
We thank Thee, Lord.

Because the Saviour of us all
Lay with the cattle in the stall,
Because the Great came to the small,
We thank Thee, Lord.

Rita F. Snowden

We open our treasures and our gifts;
And some of it is gold,
And some is frankincense,
And some is myrrh;
For some has come from plenty,
Some from joy,
And some from deepest sorrow of the soul.
But Thou, O God, dost know the gift is love,
Our pledge of peace, our promise of good will.
Accept the gift and all the life we bring.

Herbert H. Hines

O holy Child of Bethlehem! Descend to us, we pray;
Cast out our sin, and enter in, be born in us today.

Phillips Brooks

On every trembling bud and bloom
   That cleaves the earth, a flower sword,
I see Thee come from out the tomb,
   Thou risen Lord.

In every April wind that sings
   Down lanes that make the heart rejoice;
Yea, in the word the wood-thrush brings,
   I hear Thy voice.

Lo! every tulip is a cup
    To hold Thy morning's brimming wine;
Drink, O my soul, the wonder up—
    Is it not Thine?

The great Lord God, invisible,
    Hath roused to rapture the green grass;
Through sunlit mead and dew-drenched dell
    I see Him pass.

The old immortal glory wakes
    The rushing streams and emerald hills;
His ancient trumpet softly shakes
    The daffodils.

Thou art not dead; Thou art the whole
    Of Life that quickens in the sod;
Green April is Thy very soul.
    Thou great Lord God!

Charles Hanson Towne

O Thou great God of the ages, on this glorious
Easter day we would renew our joy in the sublime
resurrection message, our faith in life eternal, our
discipleship of the living Saviour. Amen.

Charles M. Crowe

Almighty God, by whose mercy I commemorate the death of my Redeemer, grant that I may so live that His death and resurrection may lead me to eternal happiness. Help me to overcome evil habits and customs. Deliver me from evil thoughts and evil deeds. Grant me light to know my duty, and grace to do it. As the days unfold, help me to become more pure and more holy. Take not from me Thy holy spirit. Grant that I may serve Thee with diligence and confidence. Grant that when Thou dost call me home, I shall enter Thine everlasting life and happiness. For the sake of Jesus Christ our Lord, Amen.

Adapted from Samuel Johnson

My Lord, what a morning!
My Lord, what a morning!
When the stars begin to fall,
You will hear the trumpet sound,
To wake the nations underground
Standing at God's right hand,
When the stars begin to fall,
My Lord, what a morning!

Negro spiritual

For the Later Years

Eternal and most glorious God, suffer me not
so to undervalue myself as to give away my soul,
Thy soul, Thy dear and precious soul, for nothing;
and all the world is nothing, if the soul be given for
it. Preserve therefore my soul, O Lord, because it
belongs to Thee, and preserve my body because it
belongs to my soul. Thou alone dost steer my boat
through all its voyages but hast a more special care
for it, when it comes to a narrow current, or to a
dangerous fall of waters. Thou hast a care of the
preservation of my body in all the ways of my life;
but, in the straits of death, open Thine eyes wider,
and enlarge Thy Providence toward me so that no
illness or agony may shake and benumb the soul. Do
Thou so make my bed in all my sickness that, being
used to Thy hand, I may be content with any bed of
Thy making. Amen.

John Donne

How long is it since I first became a Christian?
Have I grown steadily with the years?
Was I ever further forward than I am now?
Can I measure my progress in the last ten years?

                                  five years?

                                  twelve months?
I wonder how much of life remains?
What can I do now that I couldn't do five years ago?
     Lead another man to Christ?
     Distinguish guidance from my own desires?
     Forgive those who wrong me?
     Look death in the face and be unafraid?
     Really *enjoy* an hour of prayer?
When I think of "getting on" in life, do I think of
     worldly honors?
     a larger income?
     a bigger car?
     a better job?
     or more grace?
     and more of God?
Tell me, Father, am I getting on?

W. E. Sangster

As Thou hast made the world without
     Make Thou more fair the world within;
Shine through its lingering clouds of doubt;

84

Rebuke its haunting shapes of sin;
Fill, brief or long, my granted song
    Of life with love to Thee and man;
Strike when Thou wilt the hour of rest,
    But let my last days be my best.

John Greenleaf Whittier

God be in my head,
And in my understanding;
    God be in my eyes,
And in my looking;
    God be in my mouth,
And in my speaking;
    God be in my heart,
And in my thinking;
    God be at my end,
And at my departing.

Old Sarum primer

Saviour, where'er Thy steps I see,
Dauntless, untired I follow Thee;
O let Thy hand support me still,
And lead me to Thy holy hill.

Nikolas Ludwig, Graf von Zinzendorf

Prayed by the Indians

Great Spirit, help me never to judge another until I have walked in his moccasins.

Sioux prayer

The Great Father above is a Shepherd Chief. I am His, and with Him I want not. He throws out to me a rope and the name of the rope is Love, and He draws me to where the grass is green and the water not dangerous, and I eat and lie down satisfied.

Sometimes my heart is very weak and falls down, but He lifts it up again and draws me into a good road. His name is Wonderful.

Sometime—it may be very soon, it may be longer, it may be a long, long time—He will draw me into a place between mountains. It is dark there, but I'll not draw back. I'll not be afraid, for it is there between the mountains that the Shepherd Chief will meet me, and the hunger I have felt in my heart all through this life will be satisfied. Sometimes He makes the love rope into a whip.

He spreads a table before me with all kinds of food. He puts His hand upon my head and all the tired is gone. My cup He fills till it runs over.

What I tell you is true, I lie not. These roads that are away ahead will stay with me through this life, and afterward I will go to live in the Big Tepee and sit down with the Shepherd Chief forever.

Apache version of Psalm 23

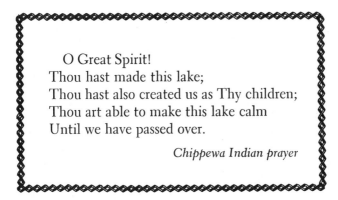

O Great Spirit!
Thou hast made this lake;
Thou hast also created us as Thy children;
Thou art able to make this lake calm
Until we have passed over.

Chippewa Indian prayer

 *From the Book*

Lord, I believe; help thou mine unbelief.

Mark 9 : 24

God be merciful to me a sinner.

The Publican, Luke 18 : 13

So teach us to number our days, that we may apply our hearts unto wisdom.

Psalm 90 : 12

Give therefore thy servant an understanding heart.

I Kings 3 : 9

O Lord, thou hast searched me, and known me. Thou knowest my downsitting and mine uprising, thou understandest my thought afar off. Thou compassest my path and my lying down, and art acquainted with all my ways. For there is not a word in my tongue, but, lo, O Lord, thou knowest it altogether. Thou hast beset me behind and before, and laid thine hand upon me.

Such knowledge is too wonderful for me; it is high, I cannot attain unto it. Whither shall I go from thy spirit? or whither shall I flee from thy presence? If I ascend up into heaven, thou art there: if I make my bed in hell, behold, thou art there. If I take the wings of the morning, and dwell in the uttermost parts of the sea; Even there shall thy hand lead me, and thy right hand shall hold me. If I say, Surely the darkness shall cover me; even the night shall be light about me. Yea, the darkness hideth not from thee; but the night shineth as the day: the darkness and the light are both alike to thee. . . .

Search me, O God, and know my heart: try me, and know my thoughts: And see if there be any wicked way in me, and lead me in the way everlasting.

Psalm 139 : 1–12, 23–24

Set a watch, O Lord, before my mouth; keep the door of my lips.

Psalm 141 : 3

Now the God of patience and consolation grant you to be likeminded one toward another according to Christ Jesus: That ye may with one mind and one mouth glorify God, even the Father of our Lord Jesus Christ.

Romans 15 : 5–6

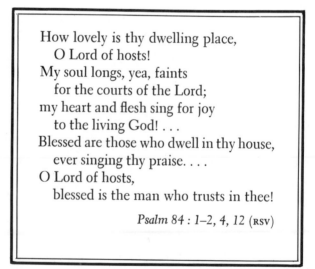

How lovely is thy dwelling place,
 O Lord of hosts!
My soul longs, yea, faints
 for the courts of the Lord;
my heart and flesh sing for joy
 to the living God! . . .
Blessed are those who dwell in thy house,
 ever singing thy praise. . . .
O Lord of hosts,
 blessed is the man who trusts in thee!

Psalm 84 : 1–2, 4, 12 (RSV)

Father, if it be possible, let this cup pass from me: nevertheless not as I will, but as thou wilt.

Jesus in Gethsemane, Matthew 26 : 39

Father, forgive them.... Into thy hands I commend my spirit.

Jesus on the cross, Luke 23 : 34, 46

Lord Jesus, receive my spirit ... Lord, lay not this sin to their charge.

Stephen when stoned, Acts 7 : 59–60

That Say Much in the Fewest Possible Words

Give me a devout heart full of affection and compassion, whereby I may pity other men's afflictions, and may have as great feeling of their miseries as if they were my own.

Augustine Baker

Give us grace, Almighty Father, so to pray as to deserve to be heard.

Jane Austen

Thou hast made us for Thyself, O Lord; and our heart is restless until it rests in Thee.

St. Augustine

My God, I wish to give myself to Thee. Give me the courage to do so.

François Fenelon

Keep open—oh, keep open . . . my eyes, my mind, my heart.

Hermann Hagedorn

Thou hast given so much to us, give us one thing more: a grateful heart.

George Herbert

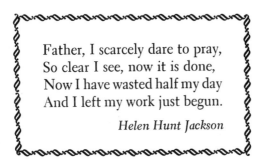

Father, I scarcely dare to pray,
So clear I see, now it is done,
Now I have wasted half my day
And I left my work just begun.

Helen Hunt Jackson

O Lord, Thou knowest that which is best for us. Let this or that be done, as Thou shalt please. Give what Thou wilt, how much Thou wilt, and when Thou wilt.

Thomas à Kempis

The things, good Lord, that we pray for,
Give us grace to labor for.

Thomas Moore

O God, help us not to despise or oppose what we cannot understand.

William Penn

Lord of Lords, grant us the good whether we pray for it or not, but evil keep from us, even though we pray for it.

Plato

O merciful Redeemer, Father and Brother, may we know Thee more clearly, love Thee more dearly, and follow Thee more nearly.

Richard, Bishop of Chichester

From silly devotions,
And from sour-faced saints,
Good Lord, deliver us.

St. Teresa of Avila

Lord, make me wiser every year,
And better every day.

Charles Lamb

Father in Heaven, when the thought of Thee wakes in our hearts, let it not waken like a frightened bird that flies about in dismay, but like a child waking from its sleep with a heavenly smile.

Søren Kierkegaard

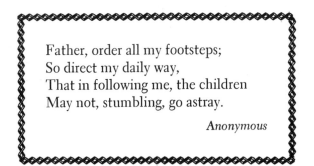

Father, order all my footsteps;
So direct my daily way,
That in following me, the children
May not, stumbling, go astray.

Anonymous

Our Father, give me the eyes to see the marks of Thy hand in the common things of life, and never let me stop pointing out those marks to others.

Dale Evans Rogers

O Lord, let us not live to be useless.

John Wesley .

Help me to love mercy, to go beyond what is acceptable in earthly society, and to do more than is expected.

J. C. Penney

The grace of the Lord Jesus Christ, and the love of God, and the communion of the Holy Ghost, be with you all. Amen.

St. Paul